Scripture Tales presents

Sam's Sacrifice

*A Story About Love
1 Corinthians 13:5*

*Written by Kate Bridges
Illustrated by Michael Larkin*

Copyright © 2016 Scripture Talk Ministries
All rights reserved.
Scripture taken from the New King James Version. Copyright © 1982 by Thomas Nelson, Inc. Used by permission. All rights reserved.
ISBN: 0986179213
ISBN-13: 978-0986179211

Dedication

This book is dedicated to my parents, who show me on a daily basis what it means to live a life of love.

1 Corinthians 13:5

"[Love] does not behave rudely, does not seek its own, is not provoked, thinks no evil."

Sam Wilson opened his eyes and sat up slowly in his bed. He stretched his hands up as far as they would go. First above his head, then down towards his toes. He grunted as he stretched--it always felt better that way.

Something was going on today, but he couldn't quite remember what it was. Hmm, what could it be?

Then, suddenly, Sam remembered. He let out a squeal and jumped out of bed in one fast hop. Today was the big day-- the day he had been looking forward to for weeks and weeks! Today was the day that they were going to have a family day at their favorite park. They were bringing their two red wagons, four bikes, balls, and jump ropes, and they would play at the park all afternoon long. They would have lots of games, swing on the swings, and explore the entire playground. And the best part of all was the surprise that Dad had accidentally given away--they were going to be allowed to bring their dog, Woof!

Even now, Sam could hear his mom in the kitchen, packing up a very special meal for their picnic lunch. She had said they would have chicken salad sandwiches with potato chips, pickles, and fruit, along with a special dessert that was a surprise for the whole family.

His parents had told him that the park was far away, and it would be a long drive to get there. It was a whole forty-five minutes away! But they had great things planned to do in the car, like playing games, eating snacks, and listening to lively music.

Oh yes. This was going to be a very, very fun day.

Just a couple of hours later, Sam and his whole family sat together in their bright red minivan as Dad carefully backed it out of their driveway and down the road. "Oh no!" cried Mom. "I forgot sunscreen! We can't possibly leave sunscreen behind--unless we want to look like lobsters by the end of the day..."

"Mama, what's a lobster?" asked Lilly, but Mom was already out the door and hurrying towards the house. "It's like a big, red crab," Christopher explained. "If we don't use sunscreen, we'll get red like that crab, and Mama won't be happy at all."

Mom appeared at the door, holding the sunscreen bottle. She climbed back in the van with a sigh of relief. "Whew!" she exclaimed, "I sure am glad I remembered that! What would we have ever done without the *sunscreen*?"

Slowly, everyone settled into their seats for the long drive. After about seven minutes of driving, Sam heard Lilly's voice beside him. "Daddy? I have to go to the bathroom."

"Oh, Lilly!" everyone cried. "We just got started!"

"Lilly," Dad said gently, "I'm wondering if you can wait a little longer before we stop?"

"Yes Daddy," she said. "I can wait."

"Here, Lilly," said Caleb, "Let's look out the window and play the alphabet game!"

The time passed happily for the children as they eagerly called out each letter. Lilly had just learned the alphabet and was having a hard time remembering which letter came after "e," but Caleb, Christopher, and Sam were good big brothers and pointed out the next letter to her as they saw it along the highway.

Finally, the children heard Dad's voice calling to them from the front seat. "We're here!"

With delighted squeals, the children craned their necks out the window to be able to see the brightly-colored playgrounds and the extra-long monkey bars and the twisting, super-sonic fast slide. "There's a tire swing!" yelled Lilly, pointing excitedly, as everyone started talking at once. The next ten minutes were mass confusion as the children piled out of the car and everyone unloaded bags and balls and coolers and water bottles, talking all the while. Woof added to the excitement as he barked and pulled on his leash and almost escaped altogether. But finally, everything was settled at the pavilion, everyone was covered in sunscreen, and the children were free to play. Well, almost free. First, Dad had to give them his safety talk. "Don't go too far, keep your shoes on, and come back for water breaks," he told the children with a smile. "Sam and Lilly, please stay close to Christopher and Caleb. Mom will be setting out the lunch, and later we'll all eat the picnic together."

"And most importantly," Mom added with a twinkle in her eye, "You'd better have fun. Got it?"

"Okay, Mom!" all the children replied cheerfully. "See you soon!"

Then off they ran, with Dad leading the way towards the playground. Woof loped behind them, wagging his tail fiercely.

The first stop was the swings, which included a thrilling contest to see who could go the very highest in the shortest amount of time. Dad gave a helping hand, pushing the children high into the air. Every once in a while, when they least expected it, Dad would surprise them by giving them a super-duper under-doggie push! The children were whooping and hollering, breathing fast, and pumping feet as hard as they could go. Woof, tied securely to a nearby tree to guard their wagons and bikes, whined anxiously as he pulled hard on his leash, watching the fun.

"I'm a bird!" yelled Sam. "I'm an airplane!" yelled Christopher. "Well, I'm a space ship!" Caleb returned. Lilly was a little more delicate. "I'm a butterfly!" she giggled.

It wasn't long before Dad, panting and wiping his forehead, announced that he was going to take a water break and go help Mom with lunch. Sam was also getting tired, so he hopped off the swing to cool down. That was when he noticed something very unusual. A little boy, who looked just about his age, was walking over to the swings with his two older siblings. What was unusual was the way he was walking. He seemed to be limping in pain. Sam couldn't help but overhear what he was saying to his siblings.

"Please slow down," the little boy was pleading. "I can't walk very fast, and I don't want to be left behind."

"But you're sooo slow," his sister retorted. "I think a turtle can walk faster than you can."

With that, she leaned over, tagged her older brother on the arm, and yelled, "Come catch me!" And the two older siblings ran off towards the jungle gym, leaving their little brother all alone. The little boy watched them sadly, his lips trembling, though he bravely tried not to cry.

Sam was just a little guy, only seven years old, but he knew what it was like to be left behind and to feel lonely. With a frown on his face, he pondered what he could do to help.

He and his siblings had planned to play freeze tag next. It was their very favorite park-day game, and he had been looking forward to it all day. But, at that moment, he realized if he chose to spend time with this little boy, they would never be able to play a game of freeze tag. Now Sam had a decision to make. Would he be willing to give up his game of tag so this little boy would not be left alone?

The Wilson siblings were hopping off the swings one by one. "Sam!" Christopher called to him. "Ready to play freeze tag?" Sam hesitated, still unsure. He looked over at the little boy, and saw he had turned and was slowly heading toward a bench on the side of the playground, with his shoulders drooping and head hanging. Suddenly, Sam had his answer.

"No," he told Christopher, "I'm going to play with that little boy over there. He can't walk very well, and his brother and sister left him all by himself."

Christopher looked over at the little boy, and a look of great sadness came into his eyes. "Maybe," he said thoughtfully, "we could find a game that all of us could play together."

And with that, he turned toward his siblings and called, "Group huddle!" which was his family's way of saying they needed to have an important meeting. Quickly gathering everyone close, Christopher explained the situation, and together they discussed what they should do.

Sam gazed longingly over at the playground. He loved to play freeze tag, probably more than anyone else in his family. But he also knew that he wanted to do the kind thing, and that was to show love to the lonely little boy who had no one to play with.

After they all agreed on their plan, Christopher led his siblings over to the little boy. "Hi," he greeted him, "my name is Christopher, and these are my brothers, Caleb and Sam, and my sister Lilly. We were wondering if you would like to play a game with us. We were thinking about having wagon races. Would you like to sit in one of the wagons?"

The little boy looked up at the siblings with wide eyes. Anyone could see he was shocked, but excited too. "Sure," he agreed slowly. Then a grin spread across his face. "That sounds like fun."

The little boy's name was Dillon, and, as it turned out, he was only a few months older than Sam. "I was in a bike wreck," he sadly told the children as they walked slowly towards Woof and the wagons. "I was going too fast, and I fell and broke my leg in two places. I had to have surgery, and I'm still learning how to walk again. It hurts an awful lot."

"I'm so sorry, Dillon," Sam told him. And the look in his eyes showed Dillon that he really meant what he had said.

Caleb helped Dillon climb up into the first wagon, and Lilly and Sam jumped into the second one. "Dillon needs a partner in his wagon," Christopher announced. "I think it should be Woof!" And before anyone could say anything else, Woof leaped up next to Dillon – much to his delight.

"On your mark, get set, GO!" yelled Caleb, and the wagons were off! The next hour passed happily with Christopher and Caleb pushing and pulling the wagons and racing each other, only taking a quick break every once in a while to catch their breath. Dillon was a very sweet boy and loads of fun to be with. He laughed and made lots of jokes. Sam knew that he had made a wonderful new friend.

"Whew!" Christopher finally cried. "I'm getting sweaty. This is a great workout, but now I need a good, long water break!"

The children flopped down on the grass, panting and laughing. Suddenly, they looked up to see Dillon's two older siblings walking briskly over to them with scowls on their faces. "Dillon, where on earth have you been?" his brother snapped. "Mom and Dad say it's time for lunch, and we've been looking all over for you!"

Roughly scooping him up into his arms, he carried Dillon off to another part of the playground.

The Wilson children walked sadly back to the pavilion for lunch. "We didn't even get to say goodbye," Sam whispered.

Mom and Dad greeted the children with cheerful smiles, but quickly became concerned when they saw their gloomy faces. "What happened?"

Christopher explained the whole story, telling them all about Dillon and his unkind siblings, while Mom and Dad listened. "And can you believe, they didn't even give us time to say goodbye?" Christopher finished angrily.

"Wow," Dad said, after pausing thoughtfully. "First of all, I want to say how proud I am of you for choosing to play with Dillon. You sacrificed your game of tag in order to play with him, but I know that it must have made his day for you to spend time with him. It sounds to me like the Lord is giving you a lesson in love. Dillon was easy to love because he was kind and cheerful, but his siblings were very hard to love, because they were rude and unthankful. Now, here's a question for you. Does the Lord ask you to love only the people who are easy to love?"

"Of course not," Sam replied thoughtfully.

"You're right, Sam," Mom said. "He tells us to love even the people who are our enemies – and even a couple of grumpy kids is *much* easier than that!"

"Only God can do that," Dad added. "So let's ask God to help us love Dillon's siblings, and do something kind for them if we see them again, okay?"

Bowing their heads, the children prayed with their parents.

"In Jesus's name, amen," Dad finished. "All right, let's eat!"

The children ate quickly. "I was *starving*!" Sam called out as he took a second sandwich from the plate, while his siblings chuckled at him. Mom revealed the surprise dessert amid squeals of delight from the two younger children, and a double whoop-roar from Caleb and Christopher. "Peanut butter chocolate chip cookies--my very favorite!" Lilly cried.

That was when Sam had an idea. "I know!" he said. "Why don't we try to find Dillon and his siblings and give them each a cookie?"

Caleb looked doubtful. "We have to give a cookie to Dillon's brother and sister too?" he asked. But then glancing at Dad, he smiled sheepishly. "Okay, Sam, that's a good idea." Thanking their mother for the wonderful lunch, the children quickly cleaned up. Then, they went running back to the playground to search for Dillon and his family.

It didn't take them long to find Dillon back at the swings with his siblings and parents. Quickly running over to the swings, the Wilson children called to the children. "Hey guys," they said, "We're about to leave, but would you like a cookie before we go?"

Dillon's brother and sister were very surprised to see the treats, and they did not say much as they each took their cookie. Dillon thanked them very kindly, though. Sam hugged Dillon, and told him that he hoped they would get to see him the next time they came to the park.

Finally, Dillon's sister spoke up. "Hey, guys," she said with a half-smile, "Thanks for playing with him. And for the cookie. That was actually really sweet."

They all smiled, and the children couldn't help but notice that the oldest brother was nodding his head in agreement. "You're welcome!" Christopher replied. "We had a lot of fun. Sorry, we didn't mean to worry you when we took him off to play with us."

"Yes, we did get a little scared when we couldn't find him," Dillon's mom admitted. "But that's all right. Looks like he had a blast."

"Time to go!" the children heard Mom and Dad calling from the side of the playground, their hands full of coolers, water bottles, and balls.

The children turned to Dillon to say one last goodbye. "Thank you, thank you for playing with me," Dillon told the children. Sam couldn't be sure, but he thought he saw a tear in Dillon's eye. Kneeling down, Dillon gave Woof a big hug, which Woof returned with a slobbery kiss.

Then the children ran toward their van, turning around every few steps to wave goodbye to their new friends. Sam knew that he would never forget Dillon and his family. But he also knew he would never forget the important lesson he had learned that day at the park--the lesson of love.

1 Corinthians 13:5

"[Love] does not behave rudely, does not seek its own, is not provoked, thinks no evil."

www.ingramcontent.com/pod-product-compliance
Lightning Source LLC
Chambersburg PA
CBHW041232040426
42444CB00002B/137